Rivers I Don't Live By

Rivers I Don't Live By

KELLY NELSON

Concrete Wolf
Poetry Chapbook Series

Copyright © 2014 Kelly Nelson
all rights reserved

ISBN 978-0-9797137-8-1

Design by Tonya Namura
using Josefin Slab

Cover art: Monica Aissa Martinez
It's all Intimate (detail)
MM on Canvas
18 x 36"
2014

Author photo: Carrie Meyer

Concrete Wolf Poetry Chapbook Series

Concrete Wolf
PO Box 1808
Kingston, WA 98346

http://ConcreteWolf.com
ConcreteWolf@yahoo.com

For my great grandmothers
Inge Røvik
Dora Beck
Karolina Ojala
and Helena Ollila
all born elsewhere and buried here

Contents

The Practice of Female Dispersal	3
Crash Land	4
Rivers I Don't Live By	5
Phoenix	6
Repairing Our Broken Furniture	7
Unsettled	8
Accumulation	9
First Trip as an Orphan	10
The birds here love crumbled walnuts, says a sign in a park in Slovenia	11
Coming Back	12
Word Count	13
Super 8, Cedar Rapids	15
If This Means Anything	16
Outpost	17
Fire Science	18
Residency	19
Home Town	20
The Geo Logic of Reincarnation	21
Notes and Acknowledgments	23
About the Author	24

Rivers I Don't Live By

The Practice of Female Dispersal

Abstract
Two million years ago, males stayed close to home, females radiated.

Methodology
Find nineteen skulls in a cave in South Africa, relatives we barely know. Test their fossil teeth for traces of minerals from the soil where their childhood food had grown. Test if those minerals match the minerals in the soil where their bones, unburied, were found.

Findings
Males died close by to where they'd grown up, while females, most of them, had left their first homes.

Discussion
When I die, my teeth will tell of Hostess Cupcakes, Frosted Flakes, chicken pot pies, Butterball turkeys, frozen fish from a bay I've never seen.

No trace will tell that I moved six hundred miles before I had any teeth. Or that I moved five hundred miles more before my second teeth pushed through. I was set in motion, like my mother and her mother and hers again—we all left home.

Crash Land

Walk off the plane.
Think: *mistake*.

Haul two bags. Find a room. The ice that won't melt
under one snow and the next wasn't shown in the color
brochures. Two years later. Tramp back onto the plane.
Think: *at least there was a river*. Stow two bags. Pick
an aisle seat.

Unstiffen dry lips
from their pinched embouchure.

Rivers I Don't Live By

If you were a landscape what would you be
I ask while we are hiking.

An emerald pool in a mossy glade, my sister says.
A snow covered alp, says her husband. A year later
they would be in therapy, two subway stops from
their Manhattan condo. I say, *I'd be a river, rocks on
both sides, water running fast enough to show white.*
A year later I would be living in a desert. The flat trail
continued dusty and unshaded, taking us through
tall, rasp-your-leg grasses. Back at the car

we would check our skin for chiggers and ticks and say,
that was a great hike.

Phoenix

Taped to my gate a notice: *we are taking your street*.
The city is taking my street

from the identical house next door clear to the end,
eighteen identical houses in all, taken to build
a highway going where they won't say. The mom
at 24196 opted for the trumpet-lessons-for-a-decade
deal for her son. Her neighbor signed over his land
for an Alaskan cruise and a pen that writes in space.
Guy next to him for a minor British title and the hand-
lettered papers to prove it. I talked to them all for the
first time, almost feel like I could miss them.

As for me, I'm last on this new cul-de-sac, shooting
scavenger birds from the high concrete walls.

Repairing Our Broken Furniture

I am trying to tell him why
I am trying to tell him what I love

about him. I've pulled out our vows that read now
like Ikea instructions in Swedish: *coarsening gore
in you-svang*—two dots atop an O sound like shut
eyes pretending to sleep—*coarsening gore in you-
svang*—the line through the O sounds like tires
skittering an ice black lake. I am sounding it out,
step by step, screw-turn-tighten, screw-turn-tighten,
a small broke-neck wrench in hand, I am trying
to tell him but he is gone, our home is gone.

The O in no scarred by pock marks.
The O in no slashed in half.

Unsettled

This furniture—futon couch, Ikea chairs, blond wood
end tables—I've posted it all on Craig's list.

My teeth, like little white storage boxes, hold the
history of everything I've eaten since those first-grade
mornings fending for myself while mom lay in bed
replaying the past. I've made the mistake again of
thinking there's a place that won't give over to routine,
a place that won't stale or stall. I have nowhere to go,
no place to be taken in, nobody waiting

but just in case I find a spark, a direction, a someone—
I want empty rooms to walk out of.

Accumulation

Novelists can't fill books without using words
they don't love.

Obligatory. Distribution. Standard. Domicile.
For the book *Material World*, photographers convinced
people to empty their houses and pose by the contents.
In Mali: metal dishes, sticks and rice, dead batteries
used by children as toys. In Iceland: crystal stemware,
floor to ceiling book cases, old pistols and several cellos.
Six months since her death, my mother's house sits
untouched. We allow it to museum—the wedding
pans, the hand-stitched dresses, the collection of wooden
Noah's Arks. *Codicil. Executrix. Residuary. Hereunto.*

Rare coins and swimming trophies in Japan.
Three dogs and ten chickens in Kuwait.

First Trip as an Orphan

The name tequila, our tour guide tells us,
can only be given to drinks made from the hearts

of blue agave grown in this region. Like Champagne,
someone says. Unlike me, I think, carting the name
of a Viking marauder into the waterless place where
I live. In the cathedral, our tour guide tells us that
relics survive without being embalmed. The word for
without here is *sin*. I am *sin* a mother, *sin* a translator,
sin a place to call home. I've become unmoored, feeling
every moment that I don't belong, yet

the crosses point in the same four directions,
the angels cast the same troubling shadows.

The birds here love crumbled walnuts, says a sign in a park in Slovenia

You pump your one speeder up the gravel path
in hope of that moment

swoosh of wings, weightless jitter—a nuthatch feeding
from your hand. To feel chosen. You stand arm out,
hand cupped, breath shallow, patient. Who appears?
Golob and vrana. Pigeon and crow. Not special enough,
you think, not special at all and so large as to scare
off the smaller, brighter, better birds. You splay your
fingers, let hope scatter, another time.

Vrana and golob step in. Seeds. Thin, brittle seeds.
They'd been hoping for walnuts.

Coming Back

What I saw was the cashier walking away
with my bag of yellow-red plums.

Follow her? Stay? Walk out of this Helsinki market
empty handed and hungry? On the boat over
from Stockholm, my mother's first language crackled
through the loud speakers. The captain did not say
milk or *mother, father* or *butter,* he did not say
I love you—the only Finnish words my mother
taught me. Our people were not city people. They felled
trees east of Oulu, shoving the trunks into dark blue
rivers. What would they know of these city streets?
What did I know of finding my way my first afternoon
in Helsinki? The cashier, blond like the daughter
I imagined I'd have, returns, the plums weighed,
the bag labeled. She rings in the price. *Sorry,* I say.
She responds in precise English

Tourists do not know. I am a tourist in my
grandmother's land. I leave with no words for goodbye.

Word Count

In the beginning   meaning 1911 when the first
                                         white man wrote it down
there were four Eskimo words for snow.
Not twenty. Not one hundred. Four.

Four o'clock, peckish, we are idling beside an order
board: twenty one names for Blizzard Treats
                        mechanically mixed
                                at Dairy Queen since 1985

            Falling Oreo Cheese Quake snow
              Choco Cherry Love snow on the ground
Over time we wanted our non-Eskimo children
to have more Eskimo words for snow.

What to call the white clumps
after microwaving a teacup poodle.
                      This never happened,
                      urban legend.

What to call the flaky fallout
from nuclear explosions.
          This did happen,
          Nevada 1950s.

The OED quietly shoves words aside to make room.
For instance, *beagle-hound* nixed leaving
just plain *beagle*. And so long *boviander*,
the mixed-race people living on the banks

of rivers in British Guyana, no longer reducible
to a single word, less articulate than snow, silent
in the face of this order board
outside the car window:

>Georgia Mud Fudge snow drift
>Xtreme Bikini Snow Blizzard
>Double Fudge drifting snow Cookie Dough
>Asbestos Cream Pie Blizzard

Snow sparkling in headlights. Flakes melting
on blacktop. We are hungry and we're idling
beside a gray plastic sign and we can't say
what it is that we want.

Super 8, Cedar Rapids

Another sour gut in a strange room. Another cluttered
plea to quit drinking, as if

slivers of morning clouds could make me keep
a promise. There have been more hills than I thought
there would be. One more day's drive and I'll be in my
mother's home town. "Why on earth would you want
to go there?" she'd ask. She knew a few lovely birds
couldn't fix the place. *Because,* I say, *without a grave
stone I need some place to remember you.* "Why not
choose a rose garden, a rose garden anywhere."
She would like that. To be remembered by beauty,
remembered by thorns.

Because, I say, *no one would know you there.*
"But that's what I want. Not to be known."

If This Means Anything

I've come looking for what these fields know
for what these railroad tracks and county highways

can tell me. A side road, I think, will give up its secrets,
so at six thirty I am walking one, white lace flowers, tall
green weeds, a man on his front porch in his underwear
drinking coffee with his wife and his dog, and I am
primed to find meaning, to assign happiness to
the bluebird perched on a wire above this side road,
six thirty, first morning walking in my mother's home
town. When I dream of my sisters, we are always in
strange houses. Is this where we can settle, on this
land where placentas have been buried? The split wood
is stacked and waiting for winter. The corn has weeks
yet to grow. And if this bluebird means anything
then it also must mean something that the driver
of a horse trailer speeding by me on the black top

whistled so loudly that my hand flew
involuntarily to my heart.

Outpost

Tell me your fire number and I'll tell you about the kid
gored by a tractor in that very same garage.

No, that happened before you were born and only the
stone-bottomed barn is left. Let's start over with a plat
map, scan the names hand lettered over rectangles
of land. About this place the history book said, *children
enjoyed playing on the flat-surfaced stumps after the
giants had been sawed and hauled to the mill.* Giants.
They can't bring themselves to say the word trees, gone
now in fence posts, in wood stoves, lying flat beneath
sixty trains a day.

Now, tell me,
tell me where you live.

Fire Science

Inspect this house—the one door, the meager windows.
Cross check the chance

of rain with the west prairie wind. *Time of day: 2 AM.*
The year: 1940. This is the house where my mother
was born. In the kitchen, her drunk father fumbles
to light a cigarette. Measure the water's speed through
the hand-drawn pump, the slim width of the table
legs. Align the hands of the clock with the spark on the
fraying rag rug.

Five people in the next room sleeping.
Now, tell me why only two made it out alive.

Residency

Your ghost has stayed to walk this untilled earth.
Field and sky. Field and sky. Field and sky.

This is everything. It is not enough. I'm standing
on a stranger's land snapping photos of a tall round
metal cage I'm guessing once held corn. I think nothing
of why corn would be caged or of why
this cage is empty. I am thinking of the show
I'll have to mount when this sabbatical is over—
photographs of implements rusting in place,
of barns leaning and fallen. How other worldly
they'll look hanging on the walls of a small gallery
on campus, read as reified nostalgia, as statements
on rural America and changing food economies.
They'll be described as

starkly haunting, liminal and spare,
same words I'd use for myself.

Home Town

We've agreed to go back. Once.
Before we're too shaky

to tromp through the woods, through the skunk
cabbage, to the stream to find whatever remains
of the statue she made at sixteen, a girl standing
with her arms crossed, a girl we left there the day
our mother moved out. We'll carry her to the car,
drive to the county park, lug her to that low lookout,
the one spot in town where you can see some place
else. No, we'll decide, we can't leave her here. We'll
head to where the main road meets the highway
at the town's only stoplight, park and wait for the bus
to the city. The driver will balk, but there are no rules
against unaccompanied statues riding the bus.
From the hood of our car, we'll wave goodbye, drink
Tab with our Entenmann's donuts

a celebration for everyone
who makes their way out.

The Geo Logic of Reincarnation

If the stories are true, most souls choose to return
to lives just led

the same old family, or right down the street, across
town, or a short ride away, returning to the people
and places they knew as if a bungee cord stretched
as they plunged into death and boinged them back to
the very same spot. Except, when they die someplace
else. The German fighter pilot gunned down over
England reincarnates as a British boy. The woman
who died on vacation reemerges in the foreign town
where she dropped to the train station floor. If we do
come back, I will, in that place in between, drink the
river water, eat the fruit, the soup that's offered,
to forget

to be surprised all over again
by where I turn up.

Notes & Acknowledgments

"The Practice of Female Dispersal": These findings come from the article "Strontium isotope evidence for landscape use by early hominids" by Sandi R. Copeland and colleagues published in the June 2011 issue of *Nature*.

Many thanks to the editors of these journals for giving these poems a home.

Arizona Literary Magazine: "Rivers I Don't Live By"
Common Ground Review: "Word Count"
Dash: "The Practice of Female Dispersal"
Eclectica: "The birds here love crumbled walnuts, says a sign in a park in Slovenia"
Kippis: "Coming Back" and "First Trip as an Orphan"
Mixed Fruit: "Outpost"
Mixitini Matrix: "Take Hold" and "Take Off"
Paddlefish: "The Geo Logic of Reincarnation"
Talking Stick: "Fire Science"
Tar River Poetry: "If This Means Anything"
2 River View: "Repairing Our Broken Furniture"
Unstrung: "Crash Land" and "Home Town"

Thanks also to the Regional Cultural Center in New York Mills, Minnesota where I was a Visiting Artist in July 2012.

About the Author

Kelly Nelson's poems have been nominated for a Pushcart Prize and for Best of the Net and have appeared in 2 *River View*, *I-70 Review*, *Watershed Review* and elsewhere. She's the recipient of a grant from the Arizona Commission on the Arts and was a Visiting Artist at the Regional Cultural Center in New York Mills, Minnesota. She holds a Ph.D. in Anthropology from Brandeis University and teaches Interdisciplinary Studies at Arizona State University. Find more at www.kelly-nelson.com.

To view some of Kelly's word installations, scan these QR codes.

www.ingramcontent.com/pod-product-compliance
Lightning Source LLC
Chambersburg PA
CBHW032110040426
42449CB00007B/1238